CLIMATE CHANGE

'Everybody talks about the weather, but nobody does anything about it,' said the American writer Mark Twain in 1897. More than 100 years later, everybody is certainly talking about the weather and climate change. From hurricanes in Brazil to floods in Bangladesh, from heat waves in France to drought in Australia, the weather is never out of the news.

But is anybody doing anything about it? The climate is changing, but why? What can we do about it, and what should we do about it? These are important questions – and perhaps there is not a lot of time to find the answers. Climate change is going to have an effect on the lives of everybody in the world.

T0344583

OXFORD BOOKWORMS LIBRARY

Factfiles

Climate Change

Stage 2 (700 headwords)

Factfiles Series Editor: Christine Lindop

BARNABY NEWBOLT

Climate Change

OXFORD UNIVERSITY PRESS

OXFORD
UNIVERSITY PRESS

Great Clarendon Street, Oxford OX2 6DP

Oxford University Press is a department of the University of Oxford.
It furthers the University's objective of excellence in research, scholarship,
and education by publishing worldwide in

Oxford New York

Auckland Cape Town Dar es Salaam Hong Kong Karachi
Kuala Lumpur Madrid Melbourne Mexico City Nairobi
New Delhi Shanghai Taipei Toronto

With offices in

Argentina Austria Brazil Chile Czech Republic France Greece
Guatemala Hungary Italy Japan Poland Portugal Singapore
South Korea Switzerland Thailand Turkey Ukraine Vietnam

OXFORD and OXFORD ENGLISH are registered trade marks of
Oxford University Press in the UK and in certain other countries

ISBN: 978 0 19 423631 7

A complete recording of this Bookworms edition of *Climate Change*
is available.

Printed in China

Word count (main text): 7,151

For more information on the Oxford Bookworms Library,
visit www.oup.com/elt/gradedreaders

ACKNOWLEDGEMENTS

With thanks to: Ann Fullick for expert science advice

Diagrams: pp 4, 7, 13, 33 by Peter Bull

The publishers would like to thank the following for permission to reproduce images:

Alamy Images p 16 (Chad, Africa); Ardea p 31 (Blue Tit feeding grubs to chicks in nest/M.Watson); Corbis
p 21 (Man hiking along Karakoram Range/Galen Rowell); Getty Images pp 2 (Krakatoa Erupts, 1888
Lithograph), 8 (Svante Arrhenius (1859 - 1927) Nobel prize winning electrochemist), 8 (Steel works,
Yorkshire/Bob Thomas), 10 (Glaciologist removing a core ice/AFP), 14 (Floods in Mumbai/AFP), 17 (Cooling
off in Valencia fountain/AFP), 19 (Man braves Typhoon Xangsane/AFP), 28 (Field of wheat/National
Geographic), 41 (Airport runway); Intergovernmental Panel on Climate Change (IPCC) Climate Change 2007:
Synthesis Report: Summary for Policy Makers page 9/Fig SPM.6 "Geographical Pattern of Surface Warming"
p 25; PA Photos pp 11 (Arctic sea ice/AP), 23 (Stranded motorists in snow/Diether Endlicher/AP), 36 (U.N.
climate conference, Kyoto/Katsumi Kasahara/AP); Panos Pictures pp 27 (Girl stands among rubbish/Jocelyn
Carlin), 37 (Resident recycling/David Rose); Science Photo Library p 11 (Arctic ice minimum extent, 2008/
NASA / GSFC / SCIENTIFIC VISUALIZATION STUDIO); Still Pictures pp viii (Cracked earth, Thailand/Nutta
Yooyean/UNEP), 12 (Water distribution point, Tanzania/Sean Sprague), 22 (Drilling hole in the ice/Nick
Cobbing/Greenpeace), 26 (Aerial view of atoll, Kuwajelein, Marshall Islands/Andre Seale/Splashdown), 31
(Polar bear feeding on caught prey/Fritz Polking), 34 (Construction site in Beijing/sinopictures/CNS),
38 (Windmills old and new/Frans Lemmens), 39 (Naturschutzkonferenz 2008/Bernd Arnold/VISUM)
Photographs of the Chacaltaya glacier on p 11 by kind permission of Bernard Francou Carbon footprint
calculator on p 40 by kind permission of www.carbonfootprint.com, copyright © Carbon Footprint Ltd 2008

CONTENTS

1 What is climate change?

The Earth is very old. It has changed often during its long life, and it is still changing. Millions of years ago, when dinosaurs like *Tyrannosaurus rex* were alive, the Earth was much warmer. There was very little ice on the land or on the sea, even in the very north or the very south of the world. And the sea was much higher than it is today.

There have been many changes since that time, sometimes to a warmer climate, sometimes to a colder one. About 20,000 years ago, for example, a time called an Ice Age began. There was ice over much of the world, and it was 3 kilometres deep over much of North America and Europe. And the sea was not as high as it is today. Our climate has changed many times, and it will change again.

Why does our climate change? Sometimes the change comes from *outside* the Earth. For example, the Earth moves around the Sun – this is called the Earth's orbit. Every few thousand years, the Earth changes its orbit around the Sun. The change happens slowly, and it brings the Earth near to the Sun or it takes it far away from the Sun. When this happens, it can finish an Ice Age – or it can start a new one.

Changes can also come from *inside* the Earth. An

Krakatoa erupting in 1883

example of this is the volcano of Krakatoa. When it erupted in 1883, the sky became dark over many countries, and stayed dark for months. And for more than a year, the Earth was 1 °C colder than before.

But now, for the very first time, *people* are changing the climate. In the year 1900, the Earth was 0.7 °C colder than it was in 2000, just one hundred years later. This change did not happen because of the Earth's orbit – it happened because of us. Some people think that this is a small change. But think about this. A change of just 5 to 7 °C can start or finish an Ice Age.

Does climate change happen quickly or slowly? The film *The Day After Tomorrow* is about a change that happens very quickly. In the film, the Earth's climate changes in only a few days, and a new Ice Age begins in the north of the world.

Can the climate change like this? Scientists think that it can – but not as quickly as this. Scientists do not always agree. Some think that the climate is changing a lot, and some think that it is changing a little. Some think that it will change quickly, and some slowly. But *all* scientists agree that climate change is happening. The important question is this: how dangerous will the change be?

Al Gore, who worked next to President Clinton of the USA between 1993 and 2001, thinks that the change will be dangerous. In his film *An Inconvenient Truth,* Al Gore describes how the Earth's climate has changed. He has talked about the dangers of climate change for more than twenty years, but is he right? Is climate change a dangerous problem? Must we do something about it? And what *can* we do?

2 How does our climate work?

Why can people live on the Earth but not on Mars or Venus? The answer is all around us: our atmosphere. Our atmosphere is made of gases that are necessary for life. The two most important gases are nitrogen (78 per

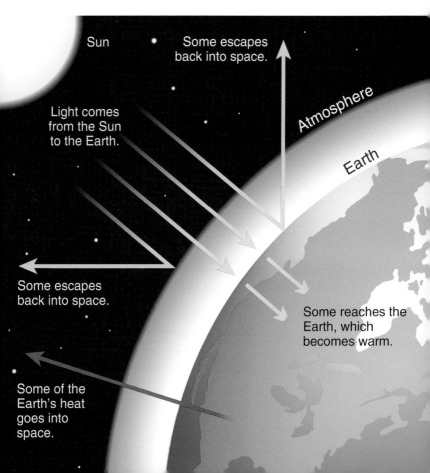

Sun

Some escapes back into space.

Light comes from the Sun to the Earth.

Atmosphere

Earth

Some escapes back into space.

Some reaches the Earth, which becomes warm.

Some of the Earth's heat goes into space.

cent) and oxygen (20 per cent). The other 2 per cent of our atmosphere is made of many other gases – and the most important of these gases for our climate is carbon dioxide (CO_2).

Our atmosphere is important because it gives us air, and we need air to live. But it has another important job. Because of our atmosphere, the Earth does not get too hot or too cold. Mars has a thin atmosphere and its temperature is about -50 °C. Venus has a thick atmosphere and its temperature is about +460 °C. The atmosphere of the Earth is somewhere between the two.

Greenhouse gases stop some heat from escaping.

Two hundred years ago in France, a scientist called Joseph Fourier had some questions about the Sun and the Earth. When the Sun shines, the Earth becomes hot. But what happens at night, he asked himself, when the Sun is not shining? Why does the Earth not lose its heat? In his garden, Fourier had a greenhouse (a building made of glass), and he put young plants in it because the air was warmer. He thought that the Earth's atmosphere was like the glass of a greenhouse. Warm air stays in a greenhouse because of the glass, and warm air stays on the Earth because of the atmosphere. We know much more about the atmosphere now than Joseph Fourier knew, but we still use his words (the 'greenhouse effect') today.

So why does the Earth not become cold? How does the greenhouse effect work?

Light from the Sun comes through the Earth's atmosphere and heats the Earth. But this heat is different from the Sun's light. Not all of this heat from the Earth can go back through the atmosphere and escape into space. There are some gases in our atmosphere that stop the heat from escaping into space. That is why these gases are called 'greenhouse gases'. The most important of them is CO_2, which stays in the atmosphere for 100 years – much longer than any other greenhouse gas!

But what stops the hot places in the world from getting hotter and hotter? And why do the cold places not get colder and colder? To answer these questions we must learn a little about the sea.

The water in the oceans moves around the world like a river. Warm water travels to cold places in the world, and makes them warmer. And cold water travels to warm places, and makes them cooler. Because there is so much water in the sea, this can make big changes to our climate. A famous example is the Gulf Stream. In the North Atlantic, the Gulf Stream carries warm water northeast from the Gulf of Mexico to Britain, Ireland and Scandinavia. The Gulf Stream brings heat to Europe; it carries fifty times more heat than all the houses, all the offices, and all the factories in the world! When the water of the Gulf Stream gets to Iceland in the north, the water becomes cold. Cold water is heavier than warm water, so

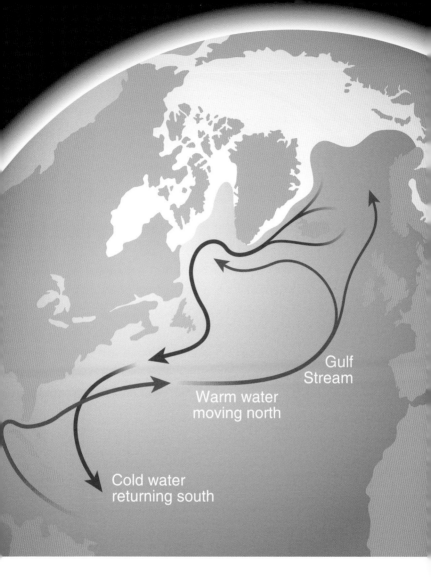

Warm water moving north

Gulf Stream

Cold water returning south

the cold water goes down under the warm water, and it goes back south.

This is what happens now. But what happens when something changes? In the next chapter, we will look at some of the changes that are happening to our atmosphere and to our seas. And we will look at the greenhouse gas CO_2.

3 Getting warmer

We do not know everything about our climate, or about climate change. But we do know two things: the Earth is getting warmer, and we are putting more CO_2 into our atmosphere every day. How do we know about these changes?

In 1896 a Swedish scientist, Svante Arrhenius, was the first person to measure the effect of CO_2 on the climate. From 1300 to 1850, the climate of Europe was much colder than it is today, but when Arrhenius was writing, the climate was changing. Europe was coming out of the 'Little Ice Age'. Arrhenius was interested

Svante Arrhenius

Smoke from 19th century factories

in this, and he thought that it was because of CO_2 in the atmosphere. If there is less CO_2, Arrhenius said, the atmosphere will become colder, and if there is more CO_2 it will become warmer. At the time, people in Europe were building more factories. The factories were burning coal and sending more CO_2 into the atmosphere. Arrhenius made new measurements. If there is 100 per cent more CO_2, he said, the atmosphere will become 5 °C warmer.

Arrhenius was nearly right. Today most scientists think that if there is 100 per cent more CO_2, the atmosphere will become 1.5 to 4.5 °C warmer. But Arrhenius thought that this would happen in 2,000 years' time – and scientists today think that it will happen in the next fifty years! Why do they think this? What is really happening?

In 1958 a scientist called Charles Keeling decided to measure the CO_2 in our atmosphere. He needed a place that was far from towns and factories. He went to Hawaii – to the top of a mountain called Mauna Loa – and he started to measure CO_2. His measurements showed that every year there is more CO_2. The CO_2 in our atmosphere has increased every year for the last fifty years.

But we can look back in time, much earlier than this. Scientists can now measure the Earth's atmosphere many thousands of years ago. To do this they cut deep holes into the ice of Antarctica and Greenland, and they take out a long, thin piece of ice. This is called an ice core. The ice at the bottom of the ice core is made from snow that fell a long time ago. When the snow froze and became ice, air stayed inside the snow. Scientists can measure the CO_2 inside this air in the ice.

Our oldest ice comes from a hole (at a place called 'Dome C' in Antarctica) that is 3,270 metres deep. The ice at the bottom of this hole came from snow that fell more than 800,000 years ago! From this ice core, we know that there is more CO_2 in our atmosphere today than at any time in the last 800,000 years. And we know that, in the last 100 years, the CO_2 in our atmosphere has increased by more than 30 per cent.

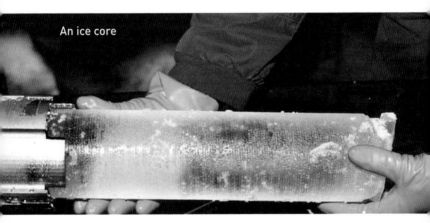

An ice core

A colder climate brings an Ice Age, but a warmer climate has the opposite effect. And that is what is happening now – the ice is melting all over the world. The ice in the glaciers of the European mountains called the Alps has been there for more than 20,000 years. But the ice in these big frozen rivers is melting, and these glaciers are now half as big as they were in 1900. In Tanzania, Africa, there is 80 per cent less snow and ice on Mount Kilimanjaro than there was in 1900, and it will all melt by 2020. The Baishui Glacier No. 1, on Mount Yulong in China, is 60 per cent smaller than it was in 1850. And in Bolivia, South America, the

Chacaltaya Glacier 1987

Chacaltaya Glacier 2007

Chacaltaya Glacier has 80 per cent less ice than it had in the 1980s.

But some of the biggest and most important changes are happening in the Arctic. Winters in Alaska and the west of Canada are nearly 4 °C warmer than in the 1950s. And in the summer the change is even bigger. In the summer of 2007, there was 20 per cent less ice covering the Arctic than in the 1970s – in other words, the Arctic has lost a piece of ice as big as the country of Egypt. Less ice covers both the land and the sea, and the ice on the sea is now less thick than it used to be – by nearly 40 per cent.

What will happen if more ice melts? This problem worries many people all over the world. But before we look at this problem, we must first look at some other changes that have already happened to our climate.

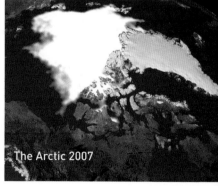

The Arctic 1970

The Arctic 2007

4   Wetter – and drier

The Earth is getting warmer and much of the Earth's ice is melting. This new water is going into the sea, and the sea level is getting higher. These changes are happening now, and they will bring many problems for the future. But other changes are happening that bring *immediate* danger to people all over the world. Changes are happening to the world's rain – *where* rain falls (or does not fall), and *how much* rain falls. Too much rain means a danger of floods; too little rain means a danger of droughts. And when there is a flood or a drought, there is less clean water to drink, and people die. In this chapter, we shall look at some of these immediate problems.

Waiting for clean water in Tanzania

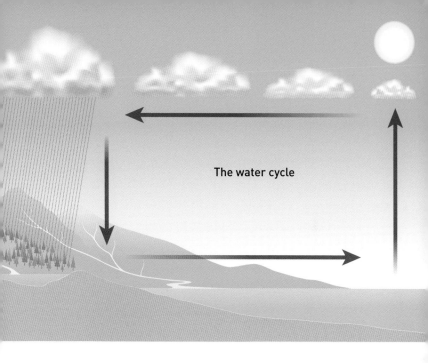

The water cycle

The sea covers 70 per cent of the Earth. Seawater is salty, and you cannot drink it. Only 3 per cent of all the water on the Earth is fresh (without salt) – and most of this fresh water is frozen in the ice of the Arctic, the Antarctic, and the world's mountains. We need water to drink, but we also need water to grow food. To grow a kilo of rice you need about 2,000 litres of water – and for animals like sheep and cows you need about 10,000 litres per kilo. Each person on the Earth needs at least 1,700,000 litres of water each year, and each year the number of people on Earth increases. So there is nothing more important to us than rain. Where does the rain come from? And is there more rain or less rain than before?

Rain comes from water in seas and rivers, and also from water that is in the land. This water evaporates in the heat of the Sun and makes water vapour – very small drops of water in the air. The water vapour goes up into the atmosphere and gets colder, and the little drops of water make clouds. When the clouds go up higher, they get colder, and the little drops of water get bigger. Then drops of rain fall, putting water back into rivers, lakes, the sea, and the land. This is called the water cycle.

Here is an example. In India, the weather is at its hottest in May. The air over the land becomes much hotter than the air over the sea. The hot air goes up very quickly, and this pulls in more air from the sea. This air, which carries water vapour from the sea, becomes a strong wind, called a monsoon. As the monsoon goes over the land, it brings heavy rains across India. Farmers need these rains to grow food. No rain means no food; but too much rain at one time means floods.

On the afternoon of 26 July 2005, Anjali Krishnan was driving to a business meeting in Mumbai, India. It started to rain, and the traffic had to stop. She waited for ten hours.

Monsoon rains in Mumbai

The rain did not stop, and she had to leave her car and try to walk home. The water in the streets of Mumbai came up to her neck, and it carried empty cars and dead cows past her. It took her two hours to get home. She was lucky, because her home was still there. But many people were less lucky. On that day, there was nearly one metre of rain, and it continued for a week. More than 50,000 people lost their homes in the floods, and 1,000 people died.

In the past, when the climate was less warm, the monsoon rains were not so heavy. But now, with a warmer climate, there are more very heavy storms in each monsoon. Scientists think that the monsoon rains will increase by more than 10 per cent during the twenty-first century. Perhaps there will be some years with little rain, but there will be more years with heavy rain and floods. And this is true for other places in the world. For many

Lake Chad

people, the twenty-first century will bring more rain, heavier rain, and more floods.

But many places in the world have the opposite problem. For them, a hotter world is a drier world. The Sahel region of Africa is south of the great, dry Sahara Desert. In this region, there is less rain than before, and one of the biggest lakes in the world has nearly disappeared. Lake Chad has lost 95 per cent of its water – and this has happened in only forty years.

So climate change is not simple. Different changes are happening in different places. But one thing is changing for everyone – the weather is making more problems. When it is hot, it is going to be hotter than before. When the wind blows, the wind will be stronger. When it rains, the rain will be heavier. In other words, the twenty-first century will bring us extreme weather.

5   Extreme weather

Something is happening to our weather. There have been big floods and long droughts, strong winds and big storms in the past. The past is full of examples of extreme weather. The difference is that now extreme weather is happening more often. Let's look at some examples.

In France, during the month of August 2003, nearly 15,000 people died because of the hot weather. The problem was not just that it was hot, but that it was so hot for so long. Weather like this is called a heat wave. In Paris the temperature during the day was above 35 °C for nine days. And on 25 August the temperature during the night did not fall below 25 °C.

Heat wave in the city

Temperatures as high as this are unusual in France, and people were not ready for days and days of very hot weather. Most of the people who died were old people, and half of them died in nursing homes. Most of the rest died at home, and only a few got to a hospital. At the beginning, the French government did not understand this new problem. 'People don't come into hospital with the words *dying of heat* on their foreheads,' said Stéphane Grossier, speaking for the French government.

Why did the hot weather happen? We know *what* happened: the Mediterranean Sea became very warm in May, and the months of June and July were unusually hot. But we do not know exactly *why* it happened. And we think that this problem is going to get worse. Scientists now think that these heat waves will increase during the twenty-first century. They think that in Central Europe, the west of the United States, and East Asia heat waves will last perhaps two days longer than they do now.

Heat waves are not the only things that are changing. Hurricanes (also called cyclones or typhoons in some parts of the world) are wind storms that start in the oceans. They can only start when the sea temperature goes above 27 °C. While they move across the sea, they need more warm water in order to grow. If they move across colder water, they get weaker. If they move across warmer water, they get stronger.

In 2004 – the year after the heat wave in France – there were a lot of hurricanes. Japan had ten, and the United States had five. For both countries, this was the largest number of big storms in one year. It was also in 2004

In a hurricane

that Brazil had Hurricane Catarina – the first hurricane to start in the South Atlantic Ocean. But the following year, 2005, was the year that got into newspapers around the world. This was the year of Hurricane Katrina, which killed more than 1,800 people and destroyed hundreds of homes in New Orleans in southern USA.

Katrina was a strong hurricane, but it was not the strongest hurricane of all. That was Hurricane Wilma, which also happened in 2005. Wilma passed across Mexico, Cuba, and Florida, killing more than sixty people and destroying hundreds of buildings. There are five categories of hurricane, from a Category 1 hurricane, which moves at 120 kilometres per hour, to a Category 5 hurricane at more than 250 kilometres per hour. Katrina and Wilma were both Category 5 hurricanes. Since 1970 we have had about the same number of hurricanes every year, but the number of Category 4 and 5 hurricanes has increased from 20 per cent to 35 per cent. Hurricanes are getting stronger!

6 Slow or sudden change?

How quickly will our climate change? This is an important question to ask, but it is very difficult to answer.

The science of climate change did not begin long ago. We did not know until 1837 about the Ice Ages of the past. It was a Swiss scientist, Louis Agassiz, who first thought of Ice Ages. He found some deep cuts in the stones of the Alps. How did they get there? His answer was that glaciers made them – glaciers that melted a long time ago. Other scientists began to think about the Ice Ages of the past. How did they begin? How did they end?

First they looked at changes from outside the Earth. They looked at the Sun, and the Earth's orbit round the Sun, and many scientists tried to measure the Earth's orbit. A scientist from Serbia, Milutin Milanković, made the final measurements about 100 years ago. The Earth's orbit changes in three different ways, he said. The first change takes about 22,000 years, the second change takes about 41,000 years, and the third takes about 100,000 years. These changes either bring the Earth closer to the Sun or they take it further away from the Sun. So, change from outside the Earth does not happen quickly!

Then they looked at changes from inside the Earth. These changes are much harder to measure because there are so many different things to look at, for example the air, the sea, the ice, and the wind. You need big computers to make these measurements. But the work of scientists like Arrhenius and Keeling taught us something new. Change from inside the Earth can happen more quickly – perhaps in hundreds of years.

We now know that climate change has happened even

Deep cuts made by glaciers

Scientists at work in Greenland

more quickly than this. Scientists have looked at ice from deep holes in Greenland that came from the end of the last Ice Age, more than 12,000 years ago. They found a very sudden change in temperature – a change of more than 10 °C in less than fifty years! How could a big change like this happen so quickly? We do not know the answer to this question, but we do know that climate change is sometimes quick and sometimes slow.

Think about this: what happens when you try to push a car along a road? If the road is flat, you can push the car slowly along the road. If the road goes down a hill, you push the car and it runs away faster and faster. Soon, you do not need to push the car at all – it keeps getting faster, and you cannot stop it. Many scientists think that we have now arrived at the top of a hill. We have changed the climate and the car is starting to go down the hill. It will be difficult to stop.

Sudden change can happen in many ways. Here is one example. There is a lot of ice in Greenland, and it is melting. If lots of cold fresh water comes into the North Atlantic, it will slow down the Gulf Stream. And when this happens, the Gulf Stream will stop carrying heat to Europe. This has happened before, a long time ago. If it happens again, it could mean very low temperatures for Europe – the opposite of a heat wave. We could see frozen rivers and icy streets in Europe, and it could happen quite soon.

Perhaps climate change will be slow – but perhaps it will be sudden. Does anyone know? Do scientists agree? We will look at this in the next chapter.

Frozen roads in Germany

7   How bad will it get?

Climate change is a global problem. All the world's governments need to work together to find answers to the problem. But they must first look at three important questions:

1 *What is happening, and why?*
2 *What can we do about the changes that are happening – now and in the future?*
3 *What can we do to put less CO_2 (and other greenhouse gases) into the atmosphere?*

In 1988 the United Nations (UN) agreed to work on this problem with the World Meteorological Organization, which studies the world's weather. They asked a group of people, called the Intergovernmental Panel on Climate Change (IPCC), to answer the three questions. The IPCC made three working groups, and they gave each group one of the three questions to answer.

By 2007, the IPCC had written four reports. Each report is made by more than 100 scientists from many different countries. Before each report is ready, more than 1,000 other scientists read it and make changes to it. Because of all this work, most scientists and most governments agree with the reports. They do not answer all the questions, because they do not know all the answers, but they give us the best answers for now.

The IPCC used nineteen different computer models

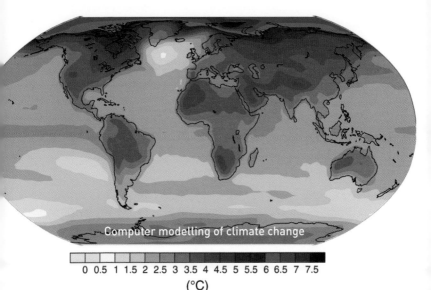

Computer modelling of climate change

0 0.5 1 1.5 2 2.5 3 3.5 4 4.5 5 5.5 6 6.5 7 7.5
(°C)

from scientists around the world to make pictures of
the world's climate in the future. Each model measured
climate change in a different way, so the answers from the
computer models were, of course, different in some ways.
But they agreed on some important changes. We will look
at just two of these changes.

1 *In the twenty-first century, the sea level will rise by
    between 28 and 43 centimetres.*

2 *In the twenty-first century, the Earth will become
    warmer by between 1.8 °C and 4 °C.*

Let's look at the first change. What will happen if the
sea rises this much? The sea is already rising. It rose by
nearly 20 centimetres during the twentieth century. In
2006 a small island called Lohachara, at the mouth of
the Ganges River in India, went under the sea. Lohachara
is the first inhabited island (an island with people living

Kuwajelein, Marshall Islands

on it) to disappear under the sea. But there are other inhabited islands that are in danger: the Maldives in the Indian Ocean, and the Marshall Islands and Tuvalu in the Pacific Ocean.

And it is not only islands that are in danger. More than 300 million people around the world live in places that are less than 1 metre above sea level. In Bangladesh half the country is less than 5 metres above sea level. There are floods every year during the monsoon, and many people die when the floods are bad. If the sea rises by 45 centimetres, Bangladesh will lose 15,000 square kilometres of land, and the homes of 5 million people will be in danger.

Now let's look at the second change. What will happen if the Earth gets nearly 2 °C warmer? We have already looked at some of the dangers: longer heat waves, bigger storms with heavier rain and stronger wind. And there are other dangers, too. More people – perhaps 90 to

200 million more people across the world – will become ill from malaria and other diseases. A lot of water will become dirty from floods, so there will be less clean water for people to drink. Many fish and other animals will be in danger (we will look at this in the next chapter.) But the biggest danger is this: think about the car running down the hill. Think about the ice in Greenland and Antarctica. Some scientists think that a temperature rise of 2 °C will melt all the ice in Greenland during the next century. That will increase the sea level – by 7 metres.

Flooding in Tuvalu

8 Is it all bad?

Is climate change bad for everyone? The short answer is: no. If you live in a cold country, the winter will be warmer than before. The plants in your garden and the food in your shops will be different. But you will still have a garden, and you will still have food. It will not be like this for everybody. Many people will not be able to change

as quickly as the climate. And think about animals and plants. How quickly can they adapt to a new climate?

In hot places there will be more dry days and less rain. The IPCC report says that food production in these places will go down by 5 per cent during the twenty-first century. But in colder places there will be more warm days and more rain. The growing season (the time of the year when plants can grow) will be longer than before. And plants need CO_2; more CO_2 is good for them. The IPCC report says that food production in the United States and Europe will increase by 5 per cent during the twenty-first

Farming in Washington, USA

century. So climate change will be good for farmers in colder countries, but it will be bad for farmers in hotter countries.

When the Arctic ice melts, it is bad for many people around the world, but in some ways it is good for the countries nearby. Russia, the United States, and other Arctic countries want the oil and gas that are in the ground under the sea, and it will be much easier to get them when the ice has melted. Without the Arctic ice (during the summer months), it will also be much easier for ships to travel across the world.

But there are many other changes that are not so good. The world is becoming warmer, and plants and animals must either adapt or die. In Vermont, in the northern United States, the winter has become warmer and the growing season is longer. This is not so good for maple trees, which give us maple syrup. Maple trees need both a cold winter and a warm summer, so now they are not doing well in Vermont. But they are doing well further north in Canada! For maple trees, like so many other plants and animals, the climate is now better in the north.

The melting ice in the Arctic is not so good for some animals. Polar bears can run on the land and swim in the water, but they need the ice when they hunt for seals. These animals live in the sea under the ice, but they make holes in the ice to get air. Polar bears wait near these holes and catch the seals when they come up for air. But in the summer months, when there is little ice, the bears cannot hunt like this, so they do not eat. And now the summer is getting longer – nearly a month longer than before.

Scientists think that we will lose 30 per cent of our polar bears in the next fifty years.

Many strange things happen because of climate change. When the sea gets warmer, turtles have more female eggs than male eggs. Nobody knows what will happen in the future. Perhaps turtles will adapt to warmer seas – or perhaps there will be fewer and fewer male turtles. In Britain and the Netherlands, there are birds called tits that eat caterpillars. This is a very important food for them when they have their young. But caterpillars become butterflies, and this is beginning to happen earlier in the year. So, when the baby tits need food, there are no more caterpillars for them to eat. Their food has flown away!

Each of these is a small problem, but many small problems make one big problem. The IPCC report says that about 25 per cent of all plants and animals are in danger if the temperature increases by more than 2 °C. Animals and plants take a long time to adapt, sometimes thousands of years. People can adapt more quickly. But are we ready to do this?

9   Carbon

The Earth is getting warmer, and the level of CO_2 in the atmosphere is rising. At Mauna Loa in Hawaii, the levels of CO_2 in the atmosphere have increased from 315 parts per million (ppm) in 1958 to 380 ppm today. And the increase of CO_2 is getting larger each year. In 1975, we put 4 gigatonnes of carbon into the atmosphere (a gigatonne is a billion tonnes). In 2008, we put more than 7 gigatonnes of carbon into the atmosphere. Where does it all go?

Life on Earth needs carbon. There is carbon in the air, the sea, and the ground. When we burn coal and oil, we put carbon back into the air as carbon dioxide. When we burn wood or cut down trees and other plants, we put carbon back into the air. But when a plant is growing, it takes carbon out of the air. Every year the level of CO_2 in the atmosphere goes up in the autumn, when plants are dying, and goes down in the spring, when plants are growing. Because of this, the large forests of the world are very important: they take CO_2 out of the air. Plants have a lot of carbon inside them, and the world's large tropical forests have nearly half of the carbon that is in the world's plants. If we cut down or burn the trees, their CO_2 will go back into the air – and there will be fewer trees to take CO_2 out of the air each spring.

We put carbon into the air, and about 25 per cent of it moves from the air into the sea. About 30 per cent goes

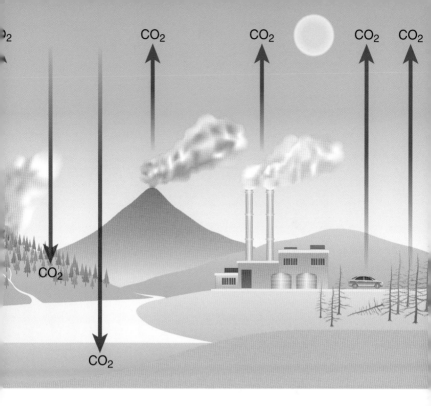

into the land, plants, or trees. The other 45 per cent goes into the atmosphere – and it stays there for a long time. But why is the level of CO_2 increasing?

We burn coal and oil to make energy for our factories, offices, and homes, and for our cars, trains, and planes. This makes about 75 per cent of the carbon that goes into the atmosphere. The other 25 per cent comes from the land. Everywhere in the world, people are building houses, offices, and roads, and cutting down plants and trees. And when plants and trees die, their carbon goes back into the atmosphere. This is where the carbon comes from. But *who* is putting it there?

Each person on Earth puts 4,600 kilos of CO_2 (or about 1,250 kilos of carbon) into the atmosphere each year. But of course this is not true. The developed countries put more greenhouse gases into the atmosphere than the

Development in Beijing, China

undeveloped countries. And many countries are developing very quickly. When they develop, they use more energy, and they put more greenhouse gases into the atmosphere. For many years, the United States has put about 20 per cent of the world's greenhouse gases into the atmosphere, which is a higher level than any other country. But now China is putting in about 20 per cent too – and China is growing very quickly.

Many countries need to develop, and they need to use energy to do this. In 2006, the International Energy Agency (IEA) asked itself this question: how much energy will all countries use in the year 2030? The answer, they think, is 100 per cent more energy than we use now – and developing countries like China and India will use 70 per cent of that new energy.

This is a global problem. It is not easy to find answers, but people have started looking for them. In the next chapter, we will look at some of these answers.

10 What are our governments doing?

The IPCC looks at problems, finds answers, and writes reports, but it cannot decide what to do. Governments have to decide. In 1992 the UN had a meeting in Rio de Janeiro, Brazil, called the Earth Summit. Here the countries of the UN looked at the first IPCC report and agreed to work together. They made a new group, the UN Framework Convention on Climate Change (UNFCCC), and they asked this new group to make a plan for their fight against climate change.

At the group's third meeting – in Kyoto, Japan, in 1997 – the UNFCCC made its plan. It is called the Kyoto Protocol. In the Kyoto Protocol, each country has a limit to its greenhouse gases. Each country that agrees to the Protocol says that it will not put more greenhouse gases into the atmosphere than its limit. Nearly all the countries in the world, 189 countries, have agreed to be at the UNFCCC meetings. But only 178 countries have agreed to the Kyoto Protocol, and it did not start until 2005. And the United States, one of the biggest producers of CO_2, has not yet agreed to the Protocol.

Will the Kyoto Protocol be the answer to our problems? Scientists think that we need to reduce CO_2 by 60 per cent if we want to stop dangerous climate change. The Kyoto

United Nations Framework Convention on Climate Change
Third Session, Conference of the Parties
Kyoto, 1 - 10 December 1997

Al Gore speaks at Kyoto

Protocol will not reduce CO_2. If all countries agree to the Protocol, CO_2 will continue to increase, but more slowly than before. So the Kyoto Protocol is just the start. What do we need to do next?

There is no quick or easy answer. To give the poorest people of the world a better life, countries need to develop, and that means using more energy. So we must learn to use energy differently. But while we are learning to do this, the Earth will get warmer. So we must also change our way of living. Our climate is going to change – if we want to live, we must change at the same time.

Countries all around the world are beginning to make changes. Hammarby Sjöstad, a part of the city of Stockholm in Sweden, has homes for 25,000 people. These homes use half as much water and energy as other Swedish homes, and half of that electricity is made using the rubbish and dirty water that comes from people's homes. In Australia, droughts have been a big problem in the twenty-first century, so at Kwinana near the city of Perth they have built their first desalination plant. (This is a factory that takes the salt out of seawater and produces fresh drinking water.) This produces 17 per cent of Perth's drinking water, and the energy for the plant also comes from wind turbines!

So some countries are beginning to make changes – and they are using energy differently too. But how can we *reduce* our greenhouse gases? We are making 7 gigatonnes of carbon a year now, and in 50 years' time we will make 14 gigatonnes of carbon a year. We need to reduce our carbon by 7 gigatonnes just to stay the same. It is a very

Hammarby Sjöstad in Stockholm

Energy from the wind

big problem. But in 2004, two scientists from Princeton University called Stephen Pacala and Robert Socolow had a good idea. 'Don't think of climate change as one problem,' they said. 'Think of it as fifteen problems with fifteen answers, because we know fifteen ways to reduce carbon. We can take seven of those answers, and for each answer, we must reduce carbon by 1 gigatonne. If we do this, we will stop the problem.'

Many people like this idea. It helps us in three ways. Firstly, we can *measure* the problem and the answers to the problem. Secondly, we can decide *how* to change – we do not need to change everything. And thirdly, we know that the answers are *possible*. They are possible because they are seven small answers, not one big answer, and also because we are doing many of them already. For example we are getting energy from wind turbines, from the Sun, and from plants, and cutting down fewer trees.

Governments are beginning to work together. They know that they must do something – but it will be difficult for them to decide which answers to use. What can we do to help?

11   What can *you* do?

We need to reduce billions of tonnes of carbon, but one person makes just over one tonne a year. So what can a single person do?

First, you can find out more. This is a short book, and it can only tell you a little about climate change. But scientists are learning new things about the climate all the time. When you know more, you can ask yourself two questions: Is climate change an important problem? Do I want to do something about it? If you can answer 'Yes' to these two questions, then you have already started to do something about it. You have started to change yourself. And that is the first thing to do.

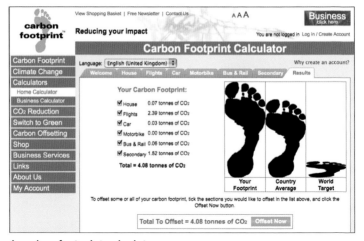

A carbon footprint calculator

Next, you can start to change other people. This is not as hard as you think. If you talk about climate change to your friends, then you will help them to change themselves. And if everyone talks about climate change, then our governments will want to do something about it. You can also help with the work of groups like Greenpeace and Friends of the Earth. Perhaps there are groups near you that are fighting against climate change.

But you can do more than talk. You can change your way of living. Ask yourself: how much carbon do *I* put into the atmosphere? (This is called your 'carbon footprint'.) You have to measure many things: your travel, your food, your clothes, your telephone, and everything in your home. And you must not forget the very big things. If your government builds a road, or your supermarket brings food from a long way away, this increases your carbon footprint. The carbon footprint of one person in one year is about 19 tonnes of CO_2 in the United States, 11 tonnes in the UK, 8 tonnes in Spain, 4 tonnes in China and 1 tonne in India. Nearly 30 per cent of this comes from travel, 20 per cent from the home, 5 per cent from food, and the rest comes from things like making clothes and building roads. It is interesting to measure your carbon footprint, but it is more important to *reduce* it.

The easiest way to reduce your carbon footprint is to use less energy. We use most energy either in the home or for travel. Think of all the things in your home, like televisions and computers, that use energy. Do you always turn them off when you are not using them? Do you use them more than you need to? Think about when you travel. Do you use a car more than you need to? Think about buying food. Does the food come from somewhere near to you, or from a long way away?

People always say that climate change is a global problem. But it is also a local problem because we can all do something about it – and we can start in our homes. It is hard to change our way of living and working. But change is like travelling on a long journey: you start in one place, and you finish in a different place. Perhaps reading this book is the start of a journey.

GLOSSARY

adapt to change the way you do things because you are in a new situation

air what you breathe

atmosphere the mixture of gases around the Earth

become to begin to be something

butterfly an insect with big coloured wings

carbon the chemical (C) that coal and diamonds are made of and that is in all living things

carbon dioxide a gas (CO_2) that people breathe out that has no colour or smell

category a group of things that are similar to each other

century a time of one hundred years

climate the normal weather conditions of a place

coal a hard black substance that comes from under the ground and is burnt to give heat

cover (*v*) to be all over something

develop to make the industries and economy of a country stronger and better

disappear to go away from a place; to stop existing

disease an illness

effect a change that happens because of something

energy the power from electricity, gas, coal etc that is used to make machines work and to make heat and light

erupt when a mountain erupts, it throws out burning rocks and smoke

extreme very strong; not ordinary or usual

evaporate to change from a liquid to a gas

farmer a person who keeps animals or grows plants for food

freeze (past **froze**) to become hard and turn to ice because of the cold

gas something like air that is not solid or liquid

global of or about the whole world

heat the quality of being hot

hunt to chase animals to catch and kill them for food

ice water that has become hard because it is frozen

increase to become bigger or more

lake a big area of water with land all round it

land the part of the Earth that is not the sea

level how high something is; the number or size of something

limit the most that is possible or allowed

maple syrup a sweet liquid that comes from the maple tree

measure to find the size or amount of something; (*n*) **measurement**

melt to become liquid after becoming warmer

model a plan that describes how something works or how something could happen

nitrogen a gas (N) that is part of the air

nursing home a small hospital where old people live and are cared for

oil a thick liquid from under the ground that we use for energy

oxygen a gas (O) in the air that people and animals need to live

part one of the pieces of something

plant something that grows in the ground

problem something difficult to understand, or find an answer for

produce to make something; (*n*) **production**

reduce to make something smaller or less

region a large area of land

report a paper written by a group of people who have looked at a particular problem

science the study of natural things; **scientist** a person who studies natural things

shine to give out light

space the area outside the Earth's atmosphere

temperature how hot or cold something is

volcano a mountain with a large opening at the top through which hot rocks, smoke, and ash are thrown into the air

wind turbine a machine that makes energy from the wind

ACTIVITIES

Before Reading

1 Match the words with the definitions.

atmosphere	A gas that people breathe out that has no colour or smell
carbon dioxide	The part of the Earth that is not the sea
century	Water that has become hard because it is very cold
climate	The mixture of gases around the Earth
ice	How hot or cold something is
land	A time of one hundred years
oil	The normal weather conditions of a place
temperature	A thick liquid from under the ground that we use for energy

2 Do you agree or disagree with these sentences? Why?

1 Climate change is the biggest problem for the Earth's future.

2 People worry and talk too much about climate change.

3 It is not too late to stop climate change.

4 Climate change has happened before and it is not a problem made by people.

5 The government needs to do a lot more about climate change.

6 We can only stop climate change if all the governments in the world work together.

ACTIVITIES

While Reading

**Read Chapter 1. Are these sentences true (T) or false (F)?
Rewrite the false ones with the correct information.**

1 Every few hundred years the Earth changes its orbit.
2 The volcano Krakatoa made the Earth 1 °C warmer.
3 The Earth in 2000 was 0.7 °C warmer than in 1900.
4 A change of only 5 °C to 7 °C can begin an Ice Age.
5 *The Day After Tomorrow* shows the climate changing slowly.
6 Only some scientists think that the climate is changing.
7 Al Gore thinks that climate change will be dangerous.

Read Chapter 2, then circle *a*, *b* or *c*.

1 Our atmosphere has mostly nitrogen and _____ in it.
   a) oxygen   b) carbon   c) carbon dioxide
2 Mars has a _____ atmosphere than the Earth.
   a) thicker   b) thinner   c) warmer
3 Fourier began to first study the atmosphere _____ years ago.
   a) fifty   b) a hundred   c) two hundred
4 Fourier said our atmosphere was like _____ in a greenhouse.
   a) plants   b) glass   c) air
5 Carbon dioxide stops _____ escaping from the Earth.
   a) oxygen   b) water   c) heat
6 The Gulf Stream moves heat to _____.
   a) Europe   b) Iceland   c) the Gulf of Mexico

Read Chapter 3. Choose the best question word for these questions, and then answer them.

How much / What / When / Where / Who / Why

1 . . . was the first scientist to measure the effect of CO_2?
2 . . . did he think the Earth would become 5 °C warmer?
3 . . . did Keeling learn from measuring CO_2?
4 . . . are scientists so interested in studying ice cores?
5 . . . can scientists find the oldest ice in the world?
6 . . . will all the ice and snow finally melt on Kilimanjaro?
7 . . . warmer are the winters in Alaska than in the 1950s?

Read Chapter 4, then rewrite these untrue sentences with the correct information.

1 The sea level on the Earth is now getting lower.
2 There is more clean water when there is a flood.
3 Only 3 per cent of the water on the Earth is salty.
4 In 2005 a drought killed many people in Mumbai.
5 Lake Chad has lost most of its fish.

Read Chapter 5. Then fill in the gaps with these numbers.

5, 9, 35, 60, 1,800, 15,000, 2003, 2005

There are now more examples of extreme weather. In August _____ there was a heat wave in France and the temperature in Paris was above _____ °C for _____ days. Nearly _____ people died.

Scientists also think that hurricanes are getting stronger. In _____, there were two Category _____ hurricanes – Hurricane Katrina, which killed over _____ people and Hurricane Wilma which killed more than _____ people.

Read Chapter 6, then circle the correct words.

1 Louis Agassiz first thought of Ice Ages when he saw cuts in *stones / glaciers* in the Alps.

2 Milanković studied the Earth's *temperature / orbit*.

3 It is easier to measure changes *inside / outside* the Earth.

4 Scientists found a *sudden / slow* change of temperature in the last Ice Age.

5 If the Gulf Stream slows down, Europe will become *cooler / warmer*.

Read Chapter 7, then match these halves of sentences.

1 Pictures of future climate change are made using . . .

2 The first inhabited island to go under the sea was . . .

3 An inhabited island in danger is . . .

4 Over 300 million people live on . . .

5 If the sea rises, 5 million people could lose their homes in . . .

6 If the Earth gets 2 °C warmer, millions of people will get . . .

7 The sea will rise by 7 metres if all the ice melts in . . .

a) Bangladesh.

b) Greenland.

c) Lohachara in India.

d) nineteen computer models.

e) malaria and other diseases.

f) Tuvalu in the Pacific Ocean.

g) land that is under 1 metre above sea level.

Read Chapter 8. Then fill in the gaps with these words.

eggs, food, gas, maple syrup, polar bears, seals

1 In future, farmers in hot countries will produce less

   _____.

2 People in Russia will find more _____.

3 Farmers in Vermont will produce less _____.

4 Polar bears will have problems catching _____.

5 The Earth will lose 30 per cent of its _____.

6 Turtles will have more female _____.

Read Chapter 9. Are these sentences true (T) or false (F)? Rewrite the false ones with the correct information.

1 In the spring the level of CO_2 in our atmosphere goes down.

2 CO_2 usually stays in the atmosphere for a short time.

3 For years China has produced the most greenhouse gases.

4 In 2030 we will use 100 per cent more energy than now.

Read Chapters 10 and 11, then answer these questions.

1 When and where was the Earth Summit?

2 What does the Kyoto Protocol try to limit?

3 Why is the Kyoto Protocol only the start of the changes?

4 How do they make electricity in Hammarby Sjöstad?

5 What is different about Pacala and Socolow's idea?

6 What is a 'carbon footprint'?

7 How big is one person's carbon footprint in India?

8 What is the biggest part of a person's carbon footprint?

9 What is the easiest way to reduce your carbon footprint?

ACTIVITIES

After Reading

1 **Match the people with the sentences. Then use the sentences to write a short description of each person. Use pronouns (*he, they*) and linking words (*and, because, but, who*).**

*Louis Agassiz, Svante Arrhenius, Joseph Fourier,
Charles Keeling, Stephen Pacala and Robert Socolow*

1 _____ was a French scientist two hundred years ago.

2 _____ were scientists at Princeton University.

3 _____ looked at the greenhouse in his garden.

4 _____ was a Swiss scientist.

5 _____ was an American scientist.

6 _____ thought the atmosphere was like greenhouse glass.

7 _____ was a scientist from Sweden.

8 _____ measured CO_2 levels on a mountain in Hawaii.

9 _____ was the first person to understand Ice Ages.

10 _____ first measured the effect of CO_2 on the climate.

11 _____ stopped thinking of climate change as one problem.

12 _____ said the climate would get much warmer in 2,000 years' time, not 50!

13 _____ began to think of climate change as fifteen problems with fifteen answers.

14 _____ showed that every year there is more CO_2 in the atmosphere.

15 _____ studied cuts in stones from the Alps.

2 Complete the crossword.

Across:

1 The area outside the Earth's atmosphere.

3 People burn this hard black substance for heat.

4 A person who grows plants or keeps animals for food.

5 When ice becomes water.

8 When something gives out light; the sun and the stars do this.

10 To chase animals to catch and kill them for food.

11 A big area of water with land all round it.

12 Carbon dioxide and oxygen are examples of this.

13 You often find this insect with coloured wings on flowers.

Down:

2 To change the way you do things because of a new situation.

3 Diamonds and coal are made of this chemical.

6 The volcano Krakatoa did this in 1883.

7 An illness; for example malaria.

9 The power from electricity, gas, oil etc.

3 **Look at these sentences about the Earth in 2050. Which ones will happen? Then write a number between 1 (will not happen) and 7 (sure to happen).**

Now write two more sentences about the Earth in 2050.

1 There will be a lot more hurricanes, floods and droughts.

2 Changes to the Gulf Stream will make Europe colder.

3 There will be no more polar bears.

4 Travel by plane will be very expensive.

5 You will pay to drive – if you drive more, you pay more.

6 Most houses will use energy from the sun.

4 **Discuss these questions in small groups.**

1 Is climate change a big or small problem for us? Why?

2 Do people think about the effect of their daily lives on climate change? Why? Why not?

3 How can governments make people think more about their carbon footprint?

4 Is it better for governments to help people to use less energy or to make them use less energy?

5 **Calculate your carbon footprint.**

• Use a website like www.footprint.wwf.org.uk or www.zerofootprint.net to calculate your carbon footprint.

• Compare it to the carbon footprint of another person in your class. Which footprint is bigger? Why?

• Discuss the best ways to reduce your carbon footprint.

ABOUT THE AUTHOR

Barnaby Newbolt worked for many years in London and in Oxford, first as a language teacher, and then as a publisher of language teaching books. During that time, he travelled to many countries, visiting schools and colleges, and speaking with teachers and students.

Now he lives and works in Cornwall, in the far south west of England, near the sea. In the morning, he is a writer; in the afternoon, he works either on the house that he is rebuilding or in the garden where he grows vegetables. In the summer, he likes to go fishing, either with a fishing rod (for small fish) or with a spear gun (for larger fish).

He is – slowly – learning how to cook, but is still better at talking and writing about food than cooking it. He enjoys playing music and singing, and is lucky that his neighbours are not close enough to hear him.

OXFORD BOOKWORMS LIBRARY

Classics • Crime & Mystery • Factfiles • Fantasy & Horror
Human Interest • Playscripts • Thriller & Adventure
True Stories • World Stories

The OXFORD BOOKWORMS LIBRARY provides enjoyable reading in English, with a wide range of classic and modern fiction, non-fiction, and plays. It includes original and adapted texts in seven carefully graded language stages, which take learners from beginner to advanced level. An overview is given on the next pages.

All Stage 1 titles are available as audio recordings, as well as over eighty other titles from Starter to Stage 6. All Starters and many titles at Stages 1 to 4 are specially recommended for younger learners. Every Bookworm is illustrated, and Starters and Factfiles have full-colour illustrations.

The OXFORD BOOKWORMS LIBRARY also offers extensive support. Each book contains an introduction to the story, notes about the author, a glossary, and activities. Additional resources include tests and worksheets, and answers for these and for the activities in the books. There is advice on running a class library, using audio recordings, and the many ways of using Oxford Bookworms in reading programmes. Resource materials are available on the website <www.oup.com/elt/gradedreaders>.

The *Oxford Bookworms Collection* is a series for advanced learners. It consists of volumes of short stories by well-known authors, both classic and modern. Texts are not abridged or adapted in any way, but carefully selected to be accessible to the advanced student.

You can find details and a full list of titles in the *Oxford Bookworms Library Catalogue* and *Oxford English Language Teaching Catalogues*, and on the website <www.oup.com/elt/gradedreaders>.

THE OXFORD BOOKWORMS LIBRARY
GRADING AND SAMPLE EXTRACTS

STARTER • 250 HEADWORDS

present simple – present continuous – imperative –
can/*cannot*, *must* – *going to* (future) – simple gerunds ...

Her phone is ringing – but where is it?

Sally gets out of bed and looks in her bag. No phone. She looks under the bed. No phone. Then she looks behind the door. There is her phone. Sally picks up her phone and answers it. *Sally's Phone*

STAGE 1 • 400 HEADWORDS

... past simple – coordination with *and*, *but*, *or* –
subordination with *before*, *after*, *when*, *because*, *so* ...

I knew him in Persia. He was a famous builder and I worked with him there. For a time I was his friend, but not for long. When he came to Paris, I came after him – I wanted to watch him. He was a very clever, very dangerous man. *The Phantom of the Opera*

STAGE 2 • 700 HEADWORDS

... present perfect – *will* (future) – *(don't) have to*, *must not*, *could* –
comparison of adjectives – simple *if* clauses – past continuous –
tag questions – *ask*/*tell* + infinitive ...

While I was writing these words in my diary, I decided what to do. I must try to escape. I shall try to get down the wall outside. The window is high above the ground, but I have to try. I shall take some of the gold with me – if I escape, perhaps it will be helpful later. *Dracula*

STAGE 3 • 1000 HEADWORDS

... should, may – present perfect continuous – *used to* – past perfect –
causative – relative clauses – indirect statements ...

Of course, it was most important that no one should see
Colin, Mary, or Dickon entering the secret garden. So Colin
gave orders to the gardeners that they must all keep away
from that part of the garden in future. *The Secret Garden*

STAGE 4 • 1400 HEADWORDS

... past perfect continuous – passive (simple forms) –
would conditional clauses – indirect questions –
relatives with *where/when* – gerunds after prepositions/phrases ...

I was glad. Now Hyde could not show his face to the world
again. If he did, every honest man in London would be proud
to report him to the police. *Dr Jekyll and Mr Hyde*

STAGE 5 • 1800 HEADWORDS

... future continuous – future perfect –
passive (modals, continuous forms) –
would have conditional clauses – modals + perfect infinitive ...

If he had spoken Estella's name, I would have hit him. I was so
angry with him, and so depressed about my future, that I could
not eat the breakfast. Instead I went straight to the old house.
Great Expectations

STAGE 6 • 2500 HEADWORDS

... passive (infinitives, gerunds) – advanced modal meanings –
clauses of concession, condition

When I stepped up to the piano, I was confident. It was as if I
knew that the prodigy side of me really did exist. And when I
started to play, I was so caught up in how lovely I looked that
I didn't worry how I would sound. *The Joy Luck Club*

BOOKWORMS · FACTFILES · STAGE 2

Rainforests

ROWENA AKINYEMI

Deep rivers, tall trees, strange animals, beautiful flowers – this is
the rainforest. Burning trees, thick smoke, new roads and cities,
dead animals, people without homes – this is the rainforest too.
To some people the rainforests mean beautiful places that you can
visit; to others they mean trees that they can cut down and sell.

Between 1950 and 2000 half of the world's rainforests
disappeared. While you read these words, somewhere in the world
people are cutting down rainforest trees. What are these wonderful
places that we call rainforests – and is it too late to save them?.

BOOKWORMS · FACTFILES · STAGE 2

The Beautiful Game

STEVE FLINDERS

Some call it football, some call it soccer, and to others it's 'the
beautiful game'. By any name, it's a sport with some fascinating
stories. There is murder in Colombia, and a game that lasts for
two days where many players never see the ball. There's the French
writer who learnt lessons about life from playing football, and
the women players who had to leave the club grounds because
'Women's football isn't nice'.

The cups, the leagues, the World Cup finals, the stars, the rules
– they're all a part of the world's favourite sport, the beautiful
game.